From the Garden into Eternity

Pearl Nsiah-Kumi

FROM THE GARDEN INTO ETERNITY
Your Choice

Pearl Nsiah-Kumi

Pearly Gates Publishing, LLC, Houston, Texas

From the Garden into Eternity

From the Garden into Eternity
Your Choice

Copyright © 2018
Pearl Nsiah-Kumi

All Rights Reserved.
No portion of this publication may be reproduced, stored in any electronic system, or transmitted in any form or by any means (electronic, mechanical, photocopy, recording, or otherwise) without written permission from the publisher. Brief quotations may be used in literary reviews.

Scripture references marked NIV and NLT are used with permission from Zondervan via Biblegateway.com. Public Domain.

ISBN 13: 978-1-947445-25-3
Library of Congress Control Number: 2018946135

For information and bulk ordering, contact:
Pearly Gates Publishing, LLC
Angela Edwards, CEO
P.O. Box 62287
Houston, TX 77205
BestSeller@PearlyGatesPublishing.com

Pearl Nsiah-Kumi

DEDICATION

This book is dedicated to God the Father for His indescribable gift, Jesus Christ, His only Begotten Son, to be our Savior, Sustainer, and coming King.

Where would we be without His grace — the grace that has brought salvation to all who will believe in Him? Had he done nothing about the sin in the Garden, everybody would have ended up in a Godless eternity…in Hell! But because Jesus lives, we shall also live.

All glory to God
— the One who will keep us
from falling away —
and bring us faultless into His presence with exceedingly great joy!

ACKNOWLEDGEMENT

Many thanks to my brother and mentor, **Dr. George Harton**, former President of the Washington Bible College and Capital Seminary, for his love, support, and encouragement in my writing endeavors. Dr. Harton, I know you are a busy man. Thank you for taking the time to edit this work! Blessings!

TABLE OF CONTENTS

DEDICATION	VI
ACKNOWLEDGEMENT	VII
INTRODUCTION	1
GOD LONGS TO HAVE A RELATIONSHIP WITH YOU	4
WHO IS GOD?	5
TRAGEDY IN THE GARDEN	7
WHERE ARE YOU?	9
YOU ARE A SINNER	13
GOD'S PLAN	16
CHRIST'S ROLE IN GOD'S REDEMPTIVE PLAN	17
YOUR RESPONSE AND ASSURANCE	21
NOW THAT YOU'VE BELIEVED	27

From the Garden into Eternity

GOD'S GOAL AND PLAN FOR YOU GOING FORWARD	29
AS A NEW CREATION AND A NEWBORN BABY	31
WHAT YOUR LIFE SHOULD BE ABOUT	33
THE BENEFITS OF SONSHIP	36
FACING HARDSHIPS	38
DON'T QUIT	45
YOUR RESPONSIBILITY IN THE BODY OF CHRIST	47
SOUL-WINNING	
(SHARING YOUR FAITH WITH OTHER PEOPLE)	59
LOOKING AHEAD	62
MEETING JESUS FACE TO FACE	67
LIVING IN ETERNITY	71
CONCLUSION	76

ABOUT THE AUTHOR	78
OTHER PUBLICATIONS BY PEARL NSIAH-KUMI	79
CONTACT PEARL NSIAH-KUMI	80

INTRODUCTION

This little book of wisdom is meant to present you with the whole counsel of God, from your birth to eternity. My goal and prayer are that you'll respond to God's love and invitation to have a personal relationship with Him and place your trust in Jesus Christ. I've put the basic information you'll need to make this important decision in one place to assist you.

But what is wisdom? *Wisdom* is the ability to apply knowledge in a positive way. It is not enough to know something or its benefits. That knowledge can be beneficial to you and your loved ones only if you apply that knowledge.

The Bible tells us, "Fear of the Lord is the foundation of wisdom" (Proverbs 9:10, NLT), and also, "Only fools say in their hearts, 'There is no God'" (Psalm 14:1, NLT). What is your position? Does God exist or does He not? What you believe about God will never change who He is. Remember: The Bible calls you a fool if you believe there is no God. On the other hand, if you believe in God's existence, how has that knowledge helped you? What difference has that knowledge made in your life? It's not enough to believe He exists; allow that knowledge to work in your favor. Start by getting to know Him in a personal way, and that will lead to your fear (reverence) of Him. The purpose of this book is to help you get to a point in your life where you appreciate God's wisdom.

GOD LONGS TO HAVE A RELATIONSHIP WITH YOU

God already knows you. He knows everything about you, including the number of hairs on your head. He sees your heart and thoughts, and knows every evil thought you have. In spite of all that, He wants to have a relationship with you. He wants you to know Him and to desire Him as much as He desires you.

By the end of the book, you'll have discovered who God is, who you are, and that man's ongoing relationship with God has always been His number one plan for mankind. You'll also learn that although you might now know it, cultivating this relationship with God is your number one need—because your life depends on it.

WHO IS GOD?

This is an excellent question because although there's only one correct answer to it, many people think God is something other than who He really is.

So, who is God?

In the beginning of time, God already existed (see Genesis 1:1). With the exception of man, He created everything by calling it into existence with the words, "Let there be…" (see Genesis 1:3-25). Then, He created man and woman in His own image. He created man first, from the dust of the earth, and breathed the breath of life into him, thus making him a living soul. Then, He created woman from man (see Genesis 1:27; 2:21-22). God was satisfied with His beautiful creation. He was—and IS—Lord of it all! Therefore, He is your Lord.

Next, God gave man dominion over all His creation and even authorized man to name each type of creation whatever he wished. He placed the first couple in the Garden of Eden, to take care of it and eat freely of the fruits for food. Only one tree, the Tree of Knowledge of Good and Evil, was off-limits to the couple (see Genesis 2:16). God clearly stated what the consequences would be for disobedience regarding that tree: "…if you eat its fruit, you are sure to die" (see Genesis 2:17). God also charged them to be fruitful and multiply: "Be fruitful and multiply. Fill the earth and govern it. Reign over the fish in the sea, the birds in the sky, and all the animals that scurry along the ground" (Genesis 1:28, NLT).

TRAGEDY IN THE GARDEN

Satan, God's rival, desiring to destroy the relationship between God and man, deceived the woman by misrepresenting the Word of God. She believed the devil's lies and ate fruit from the forbidden tree. She also offered it to her husband, who also ate it. That day, they DIED a spiritual death (separation from God) and positioned themselves for physical death down the road.

Are you wondering how Satan accomplished his goal? Well, he started by sowing doubt in Eve's mind as to what God had said. He followed that with refuting God's Word and suggesting the benefits that could result from their disobedience. He said, "You will not surely die. God knows that your eyes will be opened as soon as you eat it, as you will be like God, knowing both good and evil" (Genesis 3:4-5, NLT). Man disobeyed God, and the man died! That was a tragedy, indeed!

WHERE ARE YOU?

After the tragedy in the Garden, God dropped by in the cool of the evening, as was His routine, to chat with the couple, but they were nowhere to be found. Although God knew where they were, He called out to them.

"Where are you?" (Genesis 3:9, NLT).

Adam replied, "I heard you walking in the garden, so I hid. I was afraid because I was naked (Genesis 3:10, NLT).

This wasn't God's first visit to the garden, and they had always been naked. So, why did their nakedness matter all of a sudden? After all, they had taken care of that problem; they'd made themselves some "beautiful" clothes from leaves! The truth is they went into hiding because they had sinned, and sin has a way of making the sinner feel exposed.

The couple did not own up to their sin of disobedience. Instead, they went into finger-pointing mode. Adam blamed Eve, and Eve blamed the serpent who had no one else to blame. God pronounced judgment on all three right there on the spot (see Genesis 3:14-19), and then foreclosed on the Garden. They were never to return to it. Their luxury days were over; they had to go and fend for themselves with the knowledge that in addition to separation from God, they would eventually experience physical death (see Genesis 3:15-19).

From the Garden into Eternity

The Result of Their Disobedience

Satan promised the couple that their eyes would be opened as soon as they ate the fruit, and sure enough, their eyes were opened! But what did they see? Not what Satan promised: "You will be like God." They didn't feel anything like God. Instead, they saw their nakedness. The first thing they felt was guilt and shame; again, not what Satan promised.

Satan never keeps his promises! He is a liar and the father of lies! What did the devil do after he got the couple to disobey God? He didn't help them to face God's wrath! He probably has a smile on his face, knowing that he had accomplished his goal: interfering with God's plan.

The Consequences of Their Disobedience

As a result of their sin, the couple lost their privileges—the most devastating being the loss of their personal relationship with God. Sin had come to stay, and it put a separation between God and man. Sin didn't affect only the first couple; it also passed on to their descendants: ALL mankind. As proof, Cain (their oldest son) attacked and killed his brother, Abel, out of jealousy. Humanity has struggled with sin ever since.

YOU ARE A SINNER

Do you know you're a sinner? This is not a question for debate; you're a sinner, no matter how you see yourself. You're a sinner because you're a descendant of sinners. You sin because you're a sinner. You can't help it! "When Adam sinned, sin entered the world. Adam's sin brought death, so death spread to everyone, for everyone sinned" (Romans 5:12, NLT). And that's the reason the Bible makes it so clear that we're all sinners. "Everyone has sinned; we fall short of God's glorious standard" (Romans 3:23, NLT).

Would you like proof that we're born with a sin nature? Look at a young child trying to get out of trouble after doing something wrong. He just blames it on another person— one who probably doesn't even exist! He just makes up a name! Not only that, but he also expects the adults involved to believe him. How on earth did he figure out how to do that? The reason is clear: He was born with a sin nature. Sad, indeed!

If you don't believe you're a sinner, you're only deceiving yourself and not living in the truth (see 1 John 1:8). The worst part of that attitude is that you are calling God a liar (see 1 John 1:10).

If you agree that you're a sinner, however, there's no need to despair. There is hope: God has a plan to take away your sins and mend the broken relationship! He made mention of that plan right there in the Garden. He told Satan how it was going to go down. "I will cause hostility between you and the woman, and between your offspring and her offspring. He will strike your head, and you will strike his heel" (Genesis 3:15, NLT).

GOD'S PLAN

From the beginning of time, God planned to have an ongoing relationship with man. That relationship, however, was not going to be coerced. He wanted man to love Him freely and intentionally, so He gave man the freedom to choose.

Adam and Eve chose to disobey and, consequently, lost their standing with God, automatically passing that down to their descendants (you and me). In order to restore that relationship, sin had to be paid for. The only person good enough to pay for the sin of mankind was God Himself. He sent His Son Jesus to do just that.

CHRIST'S ROLE IN GOD'S REDEMPTIVE PLAN

Jesus came as a baby conceived by a virgin (Mary) through the power of the Holy Spirit. Many years before His birth, many prophets announced His coming as a human to deliver man from sin and to restore the broken relationship with God. All the details of His birth, life, and death happened as prophesied. As a man, He pleased God in all He did. He healed the sick, fed the poor, and raised the dead. In the end, Jesus died a painful, cruel death at the hands of sinners.

They spat on Him, hit Him, teased and insulted Him, and then crucified Him. The truth is that He willingly laid down His life because that was the only acceptable penalty for the sin of man. His love for mankind left

Him no other choice! This is what Jesus said: "The Father loves me because I sacrifice my life so I may take it back again. No one can take my life from me. I sacrifice it voluntarily. For I have the authority to lay it down when I want to and also to take it up again. For this is what my Father has commanded" (John 10:18, NLT).

The apostle Paul explained it to the churches in Galatia this way: "Jesus gave His life for our sins, just as God our Father planned, in order to rescue us from this evil world in which we live" (Galatians 1:4, NLT).

Why did God command the death of His own Son? The answer is clear—LOVE! "For this is how God loved the world: He gave His one and only Son, so that everyone who believes in Him will not perish but have eternal life" (John 3:16, NLT). God loves us so much, He wants to rescue us from this evil world in which we live and, instead, have us spend eternity with Him in Heaven after this life!

In short, Jesus' mission was to give us eternal life. "My purpose is to give them a rich and satisfying life" (John 10:10, NLT). Life is not truly satisfying until we have a personal relationship with God through Jesus.

The rich, popular, and super-educated (people you'd think should be happy) are really miserable if they don't know God. Riches, fame, and the like do not satisfy. The joy that comes from knowing Jesus in a personal way cannot be explained; it can only be experienced. There are poor, uneducated people in remote places who have unspeakable joy—more than most rich and famous folks. The difference is that one group has Jesus; the other doesn't.

YOUR RESPONSE AND ASSURANCE

You might not have given much thought to this in the past, but now do you understand that you're a sinner and the reason why you're a sinner? Do you understand your sins need to be paid for, but you don't qualify to do it yourself? That's why God demonstrated His love by sending His Son Jesus to die in your place.

But Jesus' death doesn't automatically take care of your sins. You have a responsibility in this. After all, you're the sinner in need of forgiveness.

Let's get the several misconceptions of how to get to Heaven out of the way:

- If you're thinking **there are other ways of getting to God**, you're mistaken. Jesus said, "I am the way, the truth, and the life. No one can come to the Father except through me" (John 14:16, NLT). Also, He says, "Look! I stand at the door and knock. If you hear my voice and open the door, I will come in, and we will share a meal together as friends" (Revelation 3:20, NLT).

- If you think **you can find favor with God by doing some good or heroic act**, you are mistaken again because the Bible says we're saved only by grace (unmerited favor): "God saved you by His grace when you believed. And you can't take credit for this; it is a gift from God. Salvation is not a reward for the good things we have done, so none of us can boast about it" (Ephesians 2:8-9, NLT). God is just; what He requires is the same for each sinner. If He bases salvation on good deeds, what will happen if there are different degrees of good deeds? Also, we're told, "God's way of making us right with Himself depends on faith" (Philippians 3:9, NLT).

❖ You might even be thinking that **belonging to a particular church or growing up in a Christian home** are reasons enough to assume you're a Christian. Please understand that none of those things make you a Christian. Nobody can get saved on behalf of another; each person must face God alone.

So, what makes you a Christian? What is your responsibility in all of this? You need to understand and admit that you're a sinner, repent, and ask God for forgiveness. He will forgive you and make you a new person (see 2 Corinthians 5:17) by giving you a heart that longs for Him and rejects sin.

I implore you to do that now because you're not promised tomorrow. This is a decision you have to make yourself in this life. If you wait much longer, it could be too late for you. No one can pray or eulogize you into Heaven. Establish your relationship with God now by placing your faith in Jesus: "Everyone who believes that Jesus is the Christ has become a child of God" (1 John 5:1, NLT). This will be your reservation for a place in

Heaven when you die or when Jesus returns—whichever happens first.

It is important to understand that salvation is not a decision to procrastinate about; rather, it is urgent. Although God doesn't want anyone to go to Hell, He is not going to wait forever for people to repent (see 2 Peter 3:9, 15). If I had died the day before I decided to follow Christ, my home in eternity would have been HELL! But thank God I repented and now, based on the Scriptures, I know I'm bound for Heaven! You can have that same assurance today. The window of opportunity will close sooner or later, but since no one knows how long it's going to stay open, the wisest thing to do is to make that decision the moment you hear the gospel. I encourage you to pause reading now and ask God for forgiveness through His Son, Jesus Christ.

NOW THAT YOU'VE BELIEVED

The New You and How to Live from Now On

I hope what you've read so far has given you cause for repentance and prompted you to place your faith in Jesus. Based on my hope that you've placed your faith in Jesus, I welcome you into the family of God (also known as the Church or the Body of Christ)! Like your siblings in the Church, you've been adopted! (See Romans 8:15-17).

You may (or may not) feel any different after you take this step, but with time, you'll begin to sense the peace of God. You will feel a sense of freedom from the burden of sin. You should, because He's promised to remove your sins from you as far as the east is from the west (see Psalm 103:12), and also that all who believe in the Son of God know in their hearts that God's testimony about Jesus is true (see 1 John 5:10).

Since you've taken this step, God wants you to know that your name is written in the Book of Life; you have a place in Heaven. His assurance is this: "I have written this to you who believe in the name of the Son of God, so that you may know [not wish, think, hope, or feel, but know] you have eternal life" (1 John 5:13, NLT). He has brought you out of darkness into light! Now, focus on the realities of Heaven and live accordingly (see Colossians 3:1-4).

GOD'S GOAL AND PLAN FOR YOU GOING FORWARD

God has a goal for your new life and a plan for you to attain it. He wants you to be like Him! This is how He expresses it: "You must be holy because I am holy" (1 Peter 1:16, NLT). Holiness is the state of being separated unto God who is holy and wants us to be like Him. Children look like their parents, so it should be no surprise that God wants His children to be like Him, which translates into exhibiting His nature: Holiness.

Being a sinner, you're probably wondering how you are going to attain the status of holiness. Jesus prayed for His followers (future followers included): "Make them holy by your truth; teach them your Word which is truth" (John 17:17, NLT). Studying the Word of God and applying it to our lives is how transformation occurs. It's a slow, ongoing process that gradually transforms us into the image of Christ. The Holy Spirit continues to teach us what we need to know because He knows the mind of God

AS A NEW CREATION AND A NEWBORN BABY

The Bible classifies you as a "new creation," which is what happened when the Holy Spirit came to live in your heart. The Bible expresses it this way: "Anyone who belongs to Christ has become a new person. The old life is gone; a new life has begun" (2 Corinthians 5:17)!

It also classifies you as a "baby in Christ," which has nothing to do with your biological age. There's a reason for this classification; you have a lot to learn to grow your faith. How are you going to learn that? The Bible tells you how: "Like newborn babies, you must crave pure spiritual milk so that you will grow into a full experience of salvation. Cry out for this nourishment, now that you have had a taste of the Lord's kindness" (1 Peter 2:2-3, NLT).

Child of God, you need to desire, hunger for, and long for the Word of God (the Bible)! What do people do when they're hungry? They eat! Jesus prayed that His followers would be taught the Word of God. That will not happen until we desire to know it and actually take the time to read, study, and meditate on it. As you continue to feed on the Word of God, you'll begin to understand the mind of God and your mind will get onto the path of gradual renewal, aligning with God's mind and enabling you to see things from His point of view and respond to situations the way He would.

WHAT YOUR LIFE SHOULD BE ABOUT

- ❖ As your life continues to be aligned with the mind and will of God, some things should gradually begin to change about you. It should start with love being the basis for how you live (see Ephesians 5:2), even love for those who disagree with you and even hate you (see Matthew 5:44-45). The second greatest commandment is this: "Love your neighbor as yourself" (Matthew 22:39, NLT). Relate to others the way you'd like to be treated. This will cause you to be kind, courteous, compassionate, helpful, and forgiving.

- ❖ Let the joy of knowing the Lord shine through all that you do. Allow joy in the Lord to be your strength in all circumstances (see Nehemiah 8:10). What should your joy be about? It should be about the fact that your sins are washed away, you've been brought out of darkness into light, adopted into the family of God, and your name has been recorded in the Lamb's Book of Life. To top all of that, Jesus is coming back soon to take you home to Heaven! Even though we do not deserve anything, He has promised to reward us for faithfulness in whatever we've done for Him.

❖ Consider what your character used to be like and ask yourself what God demands of you and what needs to change. Do any of these areas ring a bell: pride, arrogance, envy, explosive temper, scheming, sexual immorality, lying?

What should you do about them? For pride and arrogance, God says, "I hate pride and arrogance, corruption and perverse speech" (Proverbs 8:13, NLT). Also, the Scriptures say, "Let there be no sexual immorality, impurity, or greed among you. Such sins have no place among God's people… No immoral, impure, or greedy person will inherit the kingdom of Christ and of God" (Ephesians 5:3-5, NLT). In other words, as the Scriptures say, "Prove by the way you live that you have repented of your sins and turned to God" (Luke 3:8, NLT).

THE BENEFITS OF SONSHIP

As a child of God, your sins have been forgiven through Jesus Christ; you've won your battle with the evil one (see 1 John 2:13-14). Your name is written in the Book of Life (see Revelation 21:27). You're forever secure because no one can snatch you out of God's hand (see John 10:28). You don't ever have to worry about losing your salvation. You're sealed until the day of redemption.

You are also a joint-heir with Christ. You will inherit eternal life in Heaven! Just so you have no doubt about your standing as a Christian, the Bible reassures you in no uncertain terms (as I mentioned before): "I have written this to you who believe in the name of the Son of God, so that you may **know** you have eternal life" (1 John 5:13, NLT). You have a faithful representative: Jesus Christ the Righteous One. He intercedes for you before the Father (see 1 John 2:1).

You are entitled to call God "Father," and Jesus "Brother"! What an awesome thought and privilege! As a child of God, you can go into His presence any time of the day or night. His arms are open wide to receive you, comfort you, forgive and cleanse you, encourage you, and fight your battles. He never tires of seeing you or listening to you! After all, He rejoices over you with singing (see Zephaniah 3:17). Wow! God is really into His children! He dances over us and loves us more than we can ever imagine.

FACING HARDSHIPS

What are "hardships"? Two synonyms for hardship are "adversities" and "suffering." Being Christians does not shield us from these (as some erroneously think). In fact, Jesus said, "Here on earth, you will have many trials and sorrows. But take heart, because I have overcome the world" (John 16:33, NLT). Hardships, however, can come for different reasons: discipline, trials, temptation, and persecutions.

The end result of hardship endured with the right attitude is our transformation, more and more, into the image of our dear Lord and Savior Jesus Christ. God is sovereign and, therefore, involved in all these experiences. Nothing we experience takes Him by surprise. He allows them because He knows how they'll help in our character-building and, in the long run, bring Him glory.

- ❖ **Discipline:** Punishment or chastisement for wrongdoing, with the hope of correcting the offender. God our Father, who seeks that we be as holy as He is (see Ephesians 5:1), finds it needful to chastise us when the need arises. Discipline is not that unusual; our human parents do the same when needed. If a parent does not discipline his/her child but allows him/her to get away with wrongdoing, it indicates the parent doesn't care how the child turns out. God corrects us out of love, with one goal in mind: Godliness!
    - o Discipline can come in various forms: situations that affect our

health, finances, relationships, and a lot more. Any of these can lead to hardship. How should the child of God respond to hardships? Prayerfully examine your life and repent if the Spirit convicts you of anything. Then, learn from your mistake. Repentance will restore your relationship with the Father.

- A good example is King David. He committed adultery with Uriah's wife and then had Uriah killed (see 2 Samuel 11:2-15). God disciplined King David by allowing the baby to die (see 2 Samuel 12:11-14). David repented (see 2 Samuel 12:13; Psalm 51), and God restored him.

- o Also, the book of Job teaches us how we should view God's discipline: "Consider the joy of those corrected by God! Do not despise the discipline of the Almighty when you sin. For though He wounds, He also bandages. He strikes, but His hands also heal" (Job 5:17-18, NLT).

❖ **Trials/Temptations:** When we experience trials, the devil is trying to discourage us to a point where we could deny or turn our back on God. But under the same circumstance, God is testing (not tempting) us to see how much we are willing to endure for Him. It's our willingness that's in question here because His Word says He won't test us beyond our limit, but that He makes a way of escape for us (see 1 Corinthians 10:13).

- o Therefore, if we do not lean on Him to find the way of escape, then it is not His inability, but rather our unwillingness to endure that is the problem. A good example is Job. The devil wanted Job to deny and curse God, but God had confidence in Job's faith to endure—and he did, beautifully! This was Job's declaration: "Though he slays me, yet will I hope in Him..." (Job 13:15, NIV).

- ❖ Persecution: The devil uses people, entities, and even governments to bring pain and suffering to our lives because of our faith as Christians. People of different religions seem to enjoy discriminating against Christians in ways that cause pain and discomfort. Some governments make laws that affect Christians negatively. These include (but are not limited to) beatings, murders, imprisonments, and seizure of property for claiming to be followers of Jesus. In all these things, though, the Bible says we are more than conquerors (see Romans 8:37).
  - o We need to accept that Jesus was persecuted and, therefore, we shouldn't be surprised when we are persecuted (see John 15:20).

Thankfully, God gives us strength and grace to endure these things, and He uses those circumstances to grow our faith and to challenge the persecutors.

- A good example is the apostle Paul (formerly Saul of Tarsus). He persecuted Christians terribly until Jesus called him to faith and ministry.

Sometimes, persecutions come as mockery, insults, and name-calling. No matter which form you experience, lean on God for strength, courage, and deliverance.

DON'T QUIT

In our everyday lives, hardships have the tendency to make people quit out of frustration. But hardships in the Christian's life are meant to draw us closer to God and transform us into His image. God is aware of our hardships—no matter the source or reasons—and He can use them in molding our character into His likeness. That, of course, is not the devil's goal; he wants to give us reasons to disobey God and give up serving Him.

Jesus didn't quit when He faced suffering. His goal was to please the Father. He said He could have called for twelve legions of angels to fight, but He didn't. He was set on completing His mission of obeying the Father and saving mankind from sin and death (see Matthew 26:53-54). If we keep our eyes on

God and fix our hope on our eternal home—Heaven—we'll be victorious in our walk. The apostle Paul suffered so much for the gospel, but he never considered quitting. Instead, he told the Philippians, "I press on to reach the end of the race and receive the heavenly prize for which God, through Christ Jesus, is calling us" (Philippians 3:14, NLT).

We come to God by faith in Christ Jesus. We have to live the new life the same way: by faith. "Just as you accepted Christ Jesus as your Lord, you must continue to follow Him. Let your roots grow down into Him, and let your lives be built on Him; then your faith will grow strong in the truth you were taught" (Colossians 2:6-7, NLT). Like Paul, let's press on!

YOUR RESPONSIBILITY IN THE BODY OF CHRIST

In each family or firm, members have a responsibility which, if performed adequately, helps the families or firms run efficiently. Similarly, the Church—being the Body of Christ and also the family of God—has many members (us), and we each have a responsibility/role to play. We can't all be the same body part; we need all the different parts to complete the Body. The eyes are just as important as the mouth, the feet, the legs, and all other parts. We need to work together to accomplish the tasks God has assigned us as the Body. What are those tasks? God's expectations of us fall into one of the following categories: Love God, Love the Brethren, and Win Souls.

How Do We Love God?

First and foremost, we love God because He first loved us. He demonstrated that love by giving His One and only Son to die in our place. How should we love Him? His Word shows us how, and it is not by stating that we love Him, but by our actions that demonstrate obedience.

The Word clearly states, "Those who obey God's Word truly show how completely they love God" (1 John 2:5, NLT) and, "If you love me, obey my commandments" (John 14:15, NLT). This means putting into practice what the Bible says. Love for God should be what drives us; it should be the motive behind everything we do. If you find you have some other motive for doing something, rethink it and repent. It shouldn't be for self-gratification, praise of men, envy, jealousy, and the like. For instance, God commands us to love our neighbor as ourselves (see Matthew 22:39). When we show kindness to another person, it shouldn't be because of what they'll do for us in return or for the praises they'll heap on us; it should be out of obedience to God because we love Him.

Likewise, our love for God can be evident through our attitude toward the world and material things. The Scriptures tell us we can't serve God and money because we'll love one above the other (see Luke 16:30). Most likely, it won't be God. We are also charged, "Do not love this world nor the things it offers you, for when you love the world, you do not have the love of the Father in you" (1 John

2:15, NLT). Let's love Him through devotion and obedience.

How Do We Love The Brethren?

The Word of God commands us to love each other. It is not a suggestion, but a command that we have to obey. Everyone who believes in the name of Jesus has been born into the family of God. We've been brought out of the darkness of sin into God's light. Hence, we need to live and walk in the light.

According to the Scriptures, not loving another brother or sister is an indication that we're still walking in darkness. "If anyone claims, 'I am living in the light,' but hates a fellow believer, that person is still in darkness" (1 John 2:9, NLT).

In addition, the world around us needs to know to whom we belong, and the most tangible way of demonstrating that is by the love we show each other. Jesus said to His disciples, "Just as you can identify a tree by its fruit, so you can identify people by their actions" (Matthew 7:20, NLT). When Jesus predicted His betrayal to His disciples, He gave them a new commandment, saying, "Love each other. Just as I have loved you, you should love each other. Your love for one another will prove to the world that you are my disciples" (John 13:34-35, NLT).

God demonstrated His love for us by meeting our need for salvation, providing His Son Jesus as a substitute to die in our place. The Scriptures tell us how to love the brethren, using God as our model: "We know what real love is because Jesus gave up His life for us. So we also ought to give up our lives for our brothers and sisters. If someone has enough money to live well and sees a brother or sister in need but shows no compassion—how can God's love be in that person?" (1 John 3:16-17, NLT). So, we love the brethren by serving, forgiving, supporting, encouraging, and rebuking in love, as the need arises.

❖ Serving Each Other

How should we serve each other? We can and should serve each other in the same way Jesus served His disciples. When He washed the disciples' feet, He told them it was to be an example for them to follow, and then He said, "Do as I have done to you" (John 13:15, NLT). This example does not mean we should go around literally washing each other's feet. It does, however, mean we should serve each other in any way as needed.

In addition, each Christian has at least one spiritual gift, meant to be exercised for the benefit of the whole Body: "He has given each one of us a special gift through the generosity of Christ" (Ephesians 4:7, NLT). The purpose of the gifts is to equip God's people to do His work and build up the Church, which is the Body of Christ, resulting in the maturity of individuals and the Body as a whole (see Ephesians 4:11-13).

❖ Forgiving Offenses

Jesus taught His disciples to forgive their offenders. "If you forgive those who sin against you, your heavenly Father will forgive you. But if you refuse to forgive others, your Father will not forgive your sins" (Matthew 6:14; Mark 11:25, NLT). Paul admonished the Church in Ephesus to be humble, gentle, and patient with each other, making allowance for each other's faults (see Ephesians 4:2; Colossians 3:13). Making allowance for each other's flaws is a way of understanding and admitting our own frailty and, as a result, not taking offenses too seriously. We need to forget and let go because, sooner or later, we could be the person who needs to be forgiven.

Refusing to address offenses in a godly manner has led to many church splits. It makes me sad when I think about it. The devil takes advantage of our disagreements and unwillingness to confront and forgive. Usually, the end result is not pretty. May God help us to do better!

❖ Supporting and Encouraging

Another area of showing love to the brethren is to pray for each other; not only for those we know personally, but for the whole Body—both locally and globally. The Church at large needs support and encouragement. We are admonished to "Keep on loving each other as brothers and sisters… Remember those in prison, as if you were there yourself. Remember also those being mistreated as if though you felt their pain in your own bodies" (Hebrews 13:1-3, NLT). Christians are being persecuted in many different places. Let's feel their pain and stress, and pray that God will sustain and encourage them.

We each have different talents and responsibilities; let's help and encourage others with the delivery of their responsibilities. For instance, your pastor has the gift of shepherding the church. What should members do to encourage him? We can and should view the delivery of all the gifts that way. We need to help each other to be diligent and effective in fulfilling them.

❖ Rebuking in Love

Rebuke is a very much-needed function in the Church. Christians are the Jesus people "see," so we need to live in the light and avoid all works of darkness. If we don't, we become the reason unbelievers want nothing to do with the Jesus we represent and even cause some Christians to stumble and fall or backslide.

Peter was a mature Christian, but when Paul noticed he was being hypocritical, he rebuked him (see Galatians 2:11-13). Love should be the reason we do whatever we do. For example, Jesus died for us out of love and obedience for the Father, and God rebukes us out of love to get and keep us on the right path.

He gives us the example of what a human father would do to correct his child.

SOUL-WINNING
(Sharing Your Faith
With Other People)

Have you ever discovered where to purchase something at a terrific discount? What did you do after you secured one for yourself? I'm sure you shared the information with family and friends. Whether they checked it out or not was not your concern. You made a point of sharing the information.

The point I am making is this: If you've experienced the love of God, please share it. Others need to know! Christians are charged with the spread of the gospel by word and deed (see Matthew 5:16; 28:19-20). Jesus died to make salvation available to all. "Everyone who calls on the name of the Lord will be saved. But how can they call on Him to save them unless they believe in Him? And how can they believe in Him if they have never heard about Him? And how can they hear about Him unless someone [you] tells them?" (Romans 10:13-14, NLT).

Soul-winning is the heart of God—the reason He sacrificed His only Son! We need to share the gospel as a number one priority; time is short, and the Lord's return is inevitable. Too many people have already died and gone to a Christ-less eternity.

Those who are still alive have an opportunity to be saved, but the window of opportunity is very narrow. Life is unpredictable; nobody knows what tomorrow holds. Let's get busy and be passionate about soul-winning! Our responsibility is to pray, share the gospel, and keep praying and encouraging until God wins the soul. The Holy Spirit is the One who does the work in an individual's heart—not us—but they need to hear the message!

LOOKING AHEAD

The world is not our home. There's an old song that rightfully refers to the world as a "temporary place we are just passing through." Our treasures are laid down somewhere beyond the blue. So, while in this world, our focus needs to be on our heavenly home. Jesus told His disciples, "I am going to prepare a place for you. When everything is ready, I will come and get you, so that you will always be with me where I am" (John 14:2-3, NLT).

What an awesome promise! It should cause us to live in anticipation of the Lord's return. Living in anticipation also demands that we stay busy about our Lord's business—living godly lives and winning souls! As glorious as our future home is going to be, we also need to understand that the Lord's return date is unknown; it will come as unexpectedly as a thief breaking into your house unannounced. "The heavens will pass away with a terrible noise... Since everything around us is going to be destroyed like this, what holy and godly lives you should live... Make every effort to be found living peaceful lives that are pure and blameless in His sight" (2 Peter 3:10-14, NLT).

Live Expectantly

Have you ever waited for something to happen? What did you do during the waiting period? Imagine for a moment that in a few months, there will be a new baby in your family. What state of mind would you be in and what would you be doing as you look forward to his or her arrival? I've been there three times, and I know many people who've gone through the same experience at least once.

The basic behavior is similar with each family. There is joy, excitement, and anticipation. The news is shared with family, friends, and anyone else who will listen. There's planning and preparation; we look ahead and purchase items that we'll need to care for the baby. We want to be prepared by the time the baby is born.

Similarly, Jesus has promised to come back and take His children to Heaven—"My Father's House," as He calls it—but He also says no one knows the time or hour of His return. This gives us cause to live expectantly.

With that in mind, how should we live? We need to be living so that when He appears, we won't be surprised or ashamed. We need to be doing what He's charged us to do (sharing our faith), living our daily lives in obedience to His Word. Above all, we need to be living with joyful anticipation.

Let's share our hope with whomever will listen. Remember: "We are citizens of Heaven, where the Lord Jesus Christ lives. And we are eagerly waiting for Him to return as our Savior" (Philippians 3:20, NLT). Also, we're reminded in the book of Titus, "For the grace of God has been revealed, bringing salvation to all people. And we are instructed to turn from ungodly living and sinful pleasures. We should live in this evil world with wisdom, righteousness, and devotion to

God, while we look forward with hope to that wonderful day when the glory of our great God and Savior Jesus Christ will be revealed" (Titus 2:11-13, NLT).

MEETING JESUS FACE TO FACE

Those who have placed their faith in Jesus for salvation are going to see Jesus someday—face to face! It's going to be through one of two scenarios:

1. Our natural lives will come to an end (death) sooner or later because of old age or poor health. If that happens, we'll appear before Jesus right away because the Scripture assures us, "We would rather be away from these earthly bodies, for then we will be at home with the Lord" (2 Corinthians 5:8, NLT).
2. The Church is raptured while we are still alive. (*Rapture* means to be caught up—all living believers will one day just disappear.) The Scripture again tells us we will be caught up with Him in the air,

together with the believers who have died prior to the rapture (see 1 Thessalonians 4:17).

No matter which scenario God allows, we'll each see Jesus face to face! How awesome!

Rewards

Why on earth should we talk about rewards? Do we deserve any such thing? No! Hopefully, we've only done what we've been assigned to do as servants. Jesus said to His disciples, "When you obey me you should say, 'We are unworthy servants who have simply done our duty'" (Luke 17:10, NLT). Knowing Jesus in a personal way and having the assurance of eternity with God in Heaven should be more than enough for us. We should be thankful that we're entrusted with responsibilities and also given the grace and ability to accomplish them. This privilege should be more than enough! Nevertheless, God has promised us special rewards when we stand before Him. For instance, rewards are promised for:

- Enduring persecution (see Matthew 5:11-12);
- Faith in God and love for all of Gods people (see Colossians 1:4-5);
- Loving and trusting God (see Psalm 91:14-16);
- Planting or watering the Word of God (sharing your faith and following up to encourage and help growth) (see 1 Corinthians 3:8);

- Self-discipline in the Christian race (see 1 Corinthians 9:24-25); and
- Faithful service to masters, bosses, etc. (see Colossians 3:22-24).

LIVING IN ETERNITY

What is "eternity"? *Eternity* is time without end! Every person who has ever lived will someday experience eternity. If you're not a child of God, you should be terrified of eternity. Many people think death ends it all, but the Bible presents a different view. The Bible teaches there is an existence after this life, and it will be in one of two places: Heaven or Hell!

Heaven

What is "Heaven"? **Heaven** is God's dwelling place, the one Jesus referred to as "My Father's House" (John 14:1, NLT). Jesus said He was going to prepare a place there and, when it's ready, He'll come back to take us there, "So that you will always be with me where I am" (John 14:3, NLT). Now, it's very clear: Heaven is God's house where believers are going to spend eternity! We'll be in our glorified bodies, of course, because our mortal bodies do not qualify for heavenly existence. Our heavenly bodies will be immortal.

Now, what is Heaven like? The best architecture here on earth will not come anywhere close in comparison to Heaven! Heaven is a square city with twelve gates guarded by twelve angels. The building materials include, but are not limited to: jasper, pure gold that's as clear as glass, precious stones, sapphire, agate, emerald, onyx, carnelian, chrysotile, beryl, topaz, jacinth, amethyst, and pearls (see Revelation 21:18-21). In addition to this unspeakable magnificence, there will be no sin, tears, death, sorrow, crying, or pain (see Revelation 21:4). There will be no temple structure (God and Jesus are the Temple). The sun and moon will not be needed, because God's glory illuminates the city (see Revelation 21:22-23).

How does one get into Heaven? By being in the Lamb's Book of Life (see Revelation 21:27). How does one get listed? By repenting of sin and believing in the name of Jesus for salvation, the One who is God's substitute for sinners. "Everyone who believes that Jesus is the Christ (Savior) has become a child of God" (1 John 5:1, NLT). Here is the assurance: "I have written this to you who believe in the name of the Son of God, so that you **may know** you have eternal life" (1 John 5:13, NLT).

Hell

Hell is the alternate place to Heaven and, by definition, it is the place of eternal fire prepared for the devil and his demons (see Matthew 25:41). It is also referred to as the "Outer Darkness", where there will be weeping and gnashing of teeth (see Matthew 8:12; 22:13; Luke 13:28), and the "Fiery Lake of Burning Sulfur", where there is torment day and night…forever and ever (see Revelation 20:10). The Bible makes it clear: "Anyone whose name was not found recorded in the Book of Life was thrown into the lake of fire" (Revelation 20:15, NLT).

Arguing about the existence of Hell will not benefit anyone because its existence is the truth. It is not going to change to accommodate disagreements. If you'd rather not go to Hell, repent of your sins and call on Jesus today for forgiveness and salvation. Please don't procrastinate. Time is running out! Any day now, you could be faced with eternity, and if it's not in Heaven, then it'll be Hell! I plead with you: As you read these words, REPENT if you've never done so.

CONCLUSION

Having read this far, I'm assuming that you know without a doubt how to become a child of God and how to maintain an ongoing relationship with Him until you see Him face to face! Please take advantage of this information; your life depends on it!

Only the fool says in his heard, "There is no God" (see Psalm 14:1). If you've been thinking there's no God, or that death ends it all, or all religions lead to Heaven, or God is too good to send anyone to Hell, then let me sadly assure you of something: You're on your way to a painful eternity.

If you don't mind going to Hell, then by all means: Do nothing different. But please, please, PLEASE: Come with me to Heaven!

There's nothing to be gained by going to Hell! God loves you and really wants you to spend eternity with Him, but He will not force you to do anything you don't want to do. He will respect and grant your wishes for eternity in Hell, but please reconsider. If your status is anything other than "Saved by grace through faith in Jesus," God is waiting for your final response.

Remember: Your *LIFE* depends on it!

ABOUT THE AUTHOR

Pearl Nsiah-Kumi is a retired Registered Nurse and Christian Author. Born in Ghana, West Africa, she has lived in Maryland (U.S.) for over 40 years. She's divorced and has three adult children, one son-in-law, and four amazing grandchildren.

In addition to writing, Pearl is also a volunteer at a Crisis Pregnancy Clinic where she ministers to women in crisis.

From the Garden into Eternity

OTHER PUBLICATIONS BY PEARL NSIAH-KUMI

****

GET ON BOARD AND STAY ON BOARD

THE LAST TRAIN AT SUNSET

TIME IS RUNNING OUT

EL TIEMPO SE ESTÁ ACABANDO
(Time Is Running Out in Spanish)

LIVING FOR JESUS UNTIL HE RETURNS

PREPARE TO MEET YOUR MAKER

YOUR MAKER IS YOUR HUSBAND

**Available in print on the web at:
www.PearlKumi.com
www.Amazon.com
www.PearlyGatesPublishing.com**

Also available in various eBook versions through www.Smashwords.com.

CONTACT PEARL NSIAH-KUMI

On the Web:

www.PearlKumi.com

Via Email:

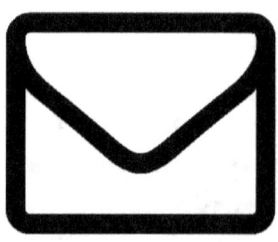

Pearl@PearlKumi.com

www.ingramcontent.com/pod-product-compliance
Lightning Source LLC
Chambersburg PA
CBHW050507120526
44588CB00044B/1685